Published by Lansdowne Press – A Division of Rigby International Ltd, 60 Milford Road, Auckland, New Zealand.

© Keith S. Clark

First Published 1983

Art Direction and Design:
  Suellen Allen
  Leonard Cobb

Typesetting:
  Linoset Services Ltd, Auckland

Printed in Hong Kong

ISBN 0-86866-071-X

AUCKLAND,
their Auckland

Written and Illustrated by K. S. Clark

Lansdowne Press
Auckland Sydney London New York

INTRODUCTION

Auckland is being so swiftly and dramatically reshaped, that soon the only places left for me to draw may be the protected historic places, or the glass and concrete container boxes that are replacing all the city's quaint minor architecture.

This collection of drawings is a record of some of the victims of Auckland's progress, and a celebration of some of its survivors. It is also a record of some of the people of those places. Only when I had finished did I realise that I had drawn and written a part of my own biography.

I arrived in Auckland from London in July 1952 when it seemed just like a boom town – all those steaks and eggs and fizzy beers!! It was so cosy and intimate and soon I knew all the local artists who taught exciting new skills such as concreting, drain-digging and homebrewing.

I hope the reader will find this an amusing book, but it is very serious about what is happening to Auckland. Changes are inevitable and often good, but we have lost so many cherished buildings and seen so many places transformed, not always for the better.

The preservation and restoration of the Customs House in Albert Street proves that people are concerned and their concern can produce results.

It would be pleasant to be able to show our grandchildren the places we have enjoyed, even if they are not all architectural classics, as they do preserve and evoke our past more poignantly than any book ever can hope to do.

Keith S. Clark

THE FERRY BUILDINGS

Completed in 1912, costing £67,944 and steam cleaned from 1957 to 1963 for £30,000, the grand old Ferry Building is rumoured to be going.

This is very sad. It is a wonderful, huge place to get lost in and has superb echoes. There seems to be hundreds of unexpected rooms where people write in big books (one feels certain), of clippers, barques, salt pork, rum and other maritime matters.

Years ago, along with several other artists, I was called to a meeting there to discuss the painting of some plaques to celebrate a visit by the Queen. The chairman rhapsodized about the Board's latest installations but most of us painted mermaids, Jack Tars with parrots and full rigged four-masters.

The Ferry Buildings have that sort of effect on people!

PRINCES WHARF

Summer picnic lunches on the steps of the wharf are one of the joys of Auckland. Office girls hitch their skirts up high and men roll down their socks and only the ambitious get back to work on time.

After two o'clock, it begins to have an 'after the holiday' look and even the gulls and the pigeons go somewhere to sleep it off.

Inside the cool-as-a-cave shelters, there is usually someone drinking from a bottle in a brown paper bag. Recently one of them offered me his bottle and when I protested that it was too early for me, he chided me that, "It's never too early to drink good sherry".

THE WATERFRONT

Another of the joys of the waterfront are the trains that rattle and clank down Quay Street to the goods sheds.

The trains' crews are weird and wonderfully dressed: football jerseys, running shorts and the occasional old army lemon-squeezer hat.

AOTEA SQUARE

The square has become the city's favourite venue for outdoor speakers, eccentrics and zealots.

The one I have drawn was a fanatical misogynist and was giving a detailed account of all the famous men who have been cheated, betrayed and ruined by "a hank of hair and a bit of bone".

The Square has attracted quite a few picturesque characters who favour military costumes of the last century. Most of them want New Zealand to "go it alone" in some fashion and one has raised a very small private army that stands around clapping at the right moments.

Japanese tourists click away at them with their cameras and waterfront workers chivvy them, but I've never seen anyone get really angry.

The Square has a large elaborate piece of metal sculpture that looks rather like the start of a big concreting job. It cost a great deal of money and I have seen people get angry about that.

I arrived at The Square at 7.30 a.m. one sunny morning to find that someone had decorated it with kitch; little garden ornaments – gnomes, rabbits and tortoises.

All around people sat reading the morning paper quite unaware of the additions.

I confess to owning a small stone tortoise paper-weight.

THE INTERNATIONAL YOGA CENTRE – NELSON STREET

The bottom half of the International Yoga Centre housed a sewing machine repair shop which you had to pass through to get upstairs where the guru instructed his classes. On a bitterly cold day, I saw this group of swamis who had obviously recently arrived in Auckland and were looking a little doubtful about this being their destination.

I wandered inside and their serenity and courtesy charmed me upstairs. It was a strangely tranquillising experience, learning asanas and breathing techniques and the Sanskrit terms for them, while the traffic rumbled along outside.

DURHAM LANE CONVENIENCES

With its elegant wrought iron work and cute little lantern, it is like a stage set – possibly for a Berthold Brecht production. By dusk, it is undeniably romantic and one Auckland painter has used it for a lovely nocturne.

A few years ago there was a notice by the door warning, "NO INTOXICATING LIQUORS ALLOWED ON THESE PREMISES"

Did any late night revellers ever say "lets go back to that beaut little loo in Durham Lane and split a bottle?"

Auckland has several splendid examples of old-time conveniences with sturdy porcelain and doors up to dungeon standards.

The Howe Street one, off K. Road, bristles with ornate iron spikery and would make a perfect set for a Jack-the-Ripper film.

I have always wondered why the Council signs directing the way to male toilets feature a top hat. Even in Europe, top hats can't be too frequent these days, and for immigrant Polynesians they must be very confusing.

THE OCCIDENTAL HOTEL
VULCAN LANE

Built in 1870 for a sailor, Edward Perkins, 'The Occ'
has a long history of attracting sportsmen and media
folk.

Many of the city's journalists drink there, standing
in little groups surrounded by the sort of people who
pride themselves on being up with the play and like
to drop the well known names of their informants.

Talk-back hosts drop in and so do a group I have
always called 'the Gangsters'. The Gangsters start
businesses and form companies and know a lot about
the law and income tax.

They are super cool and watch everybody else in the
'Occ' with an amused and slightly disdainful air.

17

THE QUEEN'S FERRY
VULCAN LANE

The 'Q.F.' 'the old 'ole in the wall', is surely the
narrowest pub in the city and maybe the darkest
too.

It has a unique attraction: a collection of bank notes
from every corner of the world displayed around the
walls.

The Gangsters usually end up at 'The Q.F.' to put
the finishing touches to their plans.

When I was drawing this picture one of them
sauntered out and came over for a talk. He was as
suave and immaculate as ever in a double-breasted
waistcoat and regimentalish tie.

He confided that he was heavily into electronics
"because nobody really knows anything about it
except a few boffins who are always looking out to
make a few bucks on the side."

THE FREYBERG STATUE
HIGH STREET

I wonder what goes through the minds of the old
digs when they come out of the High Street R.S.A.
and see their old commander facing them.

I talked with one of them who had come up from
Wellington for a reunion and he was sad, nostalgic
and rather bitter.

Another day, I eavesdropped on two young men
lunching on the seats under the statue.

'Who's that joker?' one asked.
'Dunno, some dead hero or other', was the reply.

THE MAORI ANCHOR STONES
WELLESLEY STREET
POST OFFICE

I think these Russell Clark's large Henry Moore-like carvings were the first abstract sculptures that appeared in an Auckland public place.

Under strong sunlight they become voluptuously feminine but on grey, overcast days they are primitive and menacing.

Curiously, whenever I pass them I notice women and children sitting underneath them but never men.

I mentioned this to a friend and he offered to prove me wrong, and did, but confessed he felt 'odd' and didn't elaborate.

COOK ST MARKET

Everyone tells me that Cook St. Market will be demolished this year to make way for a cultural centre. The market flowered in the sixties and a poignant reminder of those days are all the ageing hippies who call you 'man' and have adolescent children called Dylan and Milerepa.

There are stories that I hope are true:
Was it all made possible by the sale of a car?.
Did Sir Dove-Myer Robinson officiate at the presentation of the Centre of the Earth, that plaster, concrete masterpiece with the little brass Buddha plonked in the middle and the whole thing seemingly fingerpainted by someone under the influence of something?

Did Vanda really have to pull up the zips on her handcrafted form-fitting jeans with a pair of pliers?

People flock there every Saturday morning, gape at the soft sculpture, knicknacks, geegaws, buy fudge and listen to the music. Outside the Hare Krishnas chant their *mantras* and a flea market does a roaring trade.

It's still, 'all very cool, man!'

COOK STREET MARKET

If your taste in art extends to constructionism, you will be fascinated by the stalls at Cook Street Market. Most of them are not so much constructed as grown, Topsywise, from the concrete and girders. Serendipity transforms bamboo, corrugated iron, rope, parachute silk, bedspreads and any material with lots of fringes and tassels into Eastern souks. Many of the stallkeepers wear beards, brocades, harem pants, cholis and beads and burn incense in the mysterious gloom of their little stalls.

I loved to visit the man who made pipes from the claws of crabs. He squatted happily, filing, sawing and drilling under a mobile arrangement of crab claws and pipes. It was a stunning combination of aquarium and oriental bazaar.

WAH LEES –
HOBSON STREET

There are lots of Chinese provision shops in
Auckland but Wah Lees seems to be the favourite.
Over the years it has steadily expanded but
managed to avoid looking new.

There are wonderful notices attached to things "Yes
we do expect you to pick up every grain of rice and
every nut you drop!" I think one of the super polite
Wah Lee sons writes them.

One of them once trotted off to buy me an ice cream
cone when he saw me sitting drawing and
sweltering in the summer sun in Hobson Street.
Apart from everything you need to cook Chinese,
you can buy swords, musical instruments, ink stones
and brushes and superb kites.

THE HIGHER THOUGHT TEMPLE – UNION STREET

Ivan of the Floriana suggested that I should visit the Higher Thought Temple. It was cold and raining and the place looked a bit creepy under a full moon. I sat by myself for about twenty minutes until I was joined by an elderly gentleman who greeted me as 'brother' and said it looked like being a good night.

By nine o'clock about twenty of us had rolled up and things got under way. All this was a long time ago and now I wonder if it really happened as it seems, or was it the result of Ivan's vino and garlicky chicken. I have memories of people wearing sinister hoods and capes and going through a ritual involving gestures with battered old fencing foils.

There was a lot of philosophical, vaguely religious talk and we all went home at about ten thirty. Quite a few of the brothers departed on bicycles. It reminded me of scenes I had seen in Hitchcock films.

THE UNION FISH SHOP –
UNION STREET

The Union Fish Shop was next to the Higher
Thought Temple and I never found anywhere that
gave a better money's worth. Their chips were crisp
and brown, their mussels fresh, and there was
always a great pile of reading matter to browse
through while you waited.

It lingers in my memory as the archetypal Auckland
fish shop of the days when two shillings bought a
feast.

By night it glowed like a fairy palace; the bottles of
soft drinks were liquid jewels, and the trays of
squid, the strings of flounder and the unblinking fish
heads all became strangely beautiful.

DAD'S SHOP QUEEN STREET

This is my number one Auckland secondhand shop.
It is surprisingly large inside and crammed from
floor to ceiling with secondhand furniture, carpets,
mattresses and knick-knacks. There are lots of
fascinating pictures: stags at bay, wide eyed
children in sailor suits and pinafores, and Kiwis in
first world war uniforms.

I know artists who bought them for the frames and
ended up putting them on their walls.

It is pervaded by that indescribable smell of old and
vanished things – oil cloth, linoleum, feather
mattresses – *Pong du Temps Perdu!*

A demolition worker told me that it is 'on the list for
the chop'.

What a closing down sale that will be!

NO. 520 QUEEN STREET, CLOSET ARTISTS

No. 520 Queen Street was originally a gentleman's residence, complete with vestibule, dining room, study, kitchen and five bedrooms above. Later it became a doss house; then offices and now it shelters the Closet Artists.

It is a tall thin building, sitting in a garden of luxuriant weeds and ancient thickly-lichened trees. The Closet Artists have decorated it with two leering masks. At dusk, with the Chinese lanterns glowing softly inside, it looks beautiful, elegant and spooky.

I was lucky enough to overhear a marvellous snippet of conversation at an exhibition of constructions which I stupidly thought were structural renovations in progress.

An intense young man said, "I don't give a stuff about technique, craft and all that bull. What I'm after is **intensity**!"

THE HOWE STREET
GASOMETERS

Most of the quaint little colonial cottages and tiny dairies have disappeared, but the gasometers and their delicate strutting still make an arresting pattern against the sky.

A wine bar character confided to me that their rise and fall had absolutely nothing to do with the volume of gas inside but was actually a sort of barometer that registered the number of nubile young women available in the district.

Whenever I see them tumescent I look for scurrying maidens.

There used to be a dumping ground in this area that was excellent for stocking up on sinkers.

It was over-run every Saturday morning by little boys and handymen.

RUPA'S STORE
WELLINGTON STREET –
FREEMANS BAY

This, the last of the Wellington St. shops, could be the most photographed old shop in Auckland.

Time and weather has faded the advertisement for Bushells tea to the softness of a watercolour.

I have heard that officials despaired over the cash register with its pounds, shillings and pence, and the old Imperial measures scales.

Across the road, there is a supermarket and Olde Time Shoppee with beer-bottle-bottom windows to cater for the people in the smart town-houses.

PONSONBY POST OFFICE

The Ponsonby Road Post Office is over one road from the Leys Institute Library and over another from the Ponsonby Pub – the Glue Pot. A moderately swift drinker could enjoy a beer, choose a book and post a letter well inside an hour! That must be one of the swiftest historical tours in Auckland.

I have read that the Ponsonby Post Office is grossly ill-proportioned, indefensible as architecture and was fathered by the fashion for English Baroque.

It certainly is lovable in a Noddyland sort of way. The Glue Pot has the biggest public bar of any pub in Auckland and the noise has to be heard to be believed. Was it called the Glue Pot after a racehorse, or because Ponsonby ladies stayed glued to the bar when they wandered in to take a shopping break?

IVAN'S RESTAURANT
PONSONBY ROAD

For a long time 'Ivan's' was a cheap plebian place where the steak and flounder flopped over the plate and the condiments came in large bottles.

During the seventies, when soaring petrol prices made city living attractive, everyone got nostalgic for Auckland's past and started to buy and tart-up little worker's cottages. Smart, Diner's card restaurants started to mushroom on Ponsonby Road.

'Ivan's' seems to be dithering between its past and its future potential.

The old crowd can still afford the prices and the newcomers appear to find it chic – like a trip to Harlem, Pigalle or jellied eels in the East End.

RON THE POM
PONSONBY ROAD

During the years when it was considered cute to wear a T-shirt bearing the injunction to "Bash a Pom a day", Ron had the wit to open his fruit shop on Ponsonby Road.

It was a good fruit shop and stocked the fruit and vegetables Polynesians like, so Ron certainly made his peace with them.

I have known quite a few Cockneys who have set up business in Ponsonby and they have all prospered. The Ponsonby environment seems to fuel their ambition to be witty little Cockney 'sparrers' and they work hard at confounding the locals with their rhyming slang.

STEPTOES, PONSONBY ROAD

Steptoe's was a junk shop and has been replaced by an antique shop. The building is much the same but beautifully painted and the chaos of junk has given way to tasteful displays of items.

Years ago, I missed out on a lovely old wash-stand and commode, complete with flowery chamber pot – all for twenty pounds!

I wonder what it would cost if it turned up now at the antique shop. It always looked as if Steptoes bought everything offered to them. A lot of it was broken and not worth repairing, but there were treasures to be found – a lot more than there are at the places often called Serendipity.

Steptoes also had humour. I saw there (and have witnesses) a terrible reproduction of the Mona Lisa in a battered gilt frame propped against a cracked toilet bowl, and it was labelled "Original Original. One only. Ten Bob!"

THE FRIENDLY LITTLE
DAIRY OF PONSONBY ROAD

It certainly is little and friendly and it epitomises all
the other friendly little dairies in Auckland that
have been knocked down to make way for
supermarkets and used car lots.

It is favoured by the pupils of Auckland Girls'
Grammar School and by four o'clock the chatter and
giggling is frenetic.

Like all friendly little dairies, it stocks a staggering
diversity of things crammed away on the shelves in
its dark and aromatic corners.

ORSINIS, 50 PONSONBY RD

Orsinis is one of the posher, posh restaurants along Ponsonby Road's recently christened 'munchy mile'.

It is, by today's standards, a huge house with some of the finest wrought iron detail in the city.

Originally it was a physician's residence and Doctor Petit would have enjoyed marvellous views from its tower – north over the young city and west towards the Waitakere Ranges.

The Waitakere Ranges turn a deep purple blue as the sun sets and the tower is crisply and whitely silhouetted. When I worked for an advertising agency on Ponsonby Road the house became a welfare centre. Elderly gentlemen sat in the garden that faces the park where meths drinkers used to gather in little groups under the trees. Ironically, I believe the welfare centre catered for rehabilitated alcoholics.

In those days Ponsonby was rated a run down area and an advertising agency, a large successful one, was an incongruity.

When we held our meetings to hammer out strategies for selling chocolate biscuits and deodorants, the creative director inevitably flung his arm to the window which framed Doctor Petit's tower, and admonished us not to be arty or subtle but to remember, "We're talking to every joker and sheila out **there!**"

THE FLORIANA PIZZA BAR, PITT STREET

Ivan, the owner of the Floriana, had been a seaman and had spent a lot of time in Latin America. The cafes and *bodegas* inspired Ivan. "There were sausages and stuff hung up all over the flaming place" he told me, "It was colourful – romantic!"

When he invited me round the back for a vino which he kept in an enormous battered old fridge, he talked long and lyrically of those wonderful Latin American places.

He also believed in garlic, more than anyone I have ever met! Garlic annihilated the taste of everything!

As the weeks went by it became harder to thread a passage through the sausages to the counter, so the Health Department demanded that it be modified.

I published a drawing which included a policeman, and a real policeman complained that I was taking the mickey out of him. It certainly did look like him but I had never even seen him before!

The last I heard of Ivan was that he was a successful chef in London.

KARANGAHAPE ROAD

Originally named KARANGAHAPE TE ARO (track to the shellfish), then, to accommodate monolingual migrants, Fleet Street, George Street, and now K. Road.

There is a delicious story about a policeman finding a dead horse on Karangahape Road and hauling it by its hind legs to Pitt Street – which he **could** spell!

On warm summer evenings, when it is packed with Polynesians and the shops are livid with neon, it seems more like Asia than Godzone. K. Rd has strip joints, junk shops, ethnic restaurants, exciting pubs and a lot of interesting and bizarre personalities.

There are stories going round of a big development, a clean up of ancient buildings and a proliferation of malls, boutiques and all manner of profit making installations.

THE NAUGHTY SCHOOLGIRL
– PINK PUSSY CAT K. ROAD

Until a few years ago, there was always a naughty schoolgirl at the Pink Pussy Cat. As one left, another took her place and carried on the routine.

The routine was to simper, skip, fiddle with a school bag and offer a lolly to the audience as she gradually disrobed.

One naughty school girl was so convincing that she kept her costume on when she left and went home on the bus – for half fare!

It is over twenty years since Rainton Hastie set up the Pink Pussy Cat in K. Road and he has declared that his ambition now is to open up a high-class establishment – so high-class it will cost $200 to get inside the door!

Will that be part of the K. Road redevelopment?

THE PINK PUSSY CAT –
K. ROAD

The Pink Pussy was the first of the Queen City's strip joints and dates from the days when the girls wore pasties.

In 1965, Charmaine Lee's pasties came off during her show and the audience loved it so much they decided to keep it like that. The law moved in, but topless acts were found not illegal and the Pink Pussy flourished.

Out-of-town football clubs, overseas business men and office parties flocked there.

The bump and grind beat was deafening and the strobe lighting eye-piercing. A sign over the door of the old Pink Pussy said "You are now entering the wonderful world of Burlesque" and it was true. All this was long before rap parlours and peep shows. Looking back it was all provincial, boyish fun.

DAVID FLAME'S CREATIONS
K. ROAD

If you want to buy a leopard skin cat suit, a
sequined G-string or a pair of bikini pants (with or
without a crutch) David Flame's is the shop you're
looking for.

Bert the street-cleaner and an old wine bar chum
whom I have drawn, has been working this stretch
of K. Road for quite a few years, but he admits that
the Flame's erotically undressed display figures still
give him a turn when he's not quite prepared for
them.

Upstairs is the 'Naughty Knickers Coffee Bar',
where for ten dollars you can watch living girls
sashay around in The Flame Creations.

Sensibly, the establishment is next to 'The Pink
Pussy Cat'.

DANCE NIGHT AT THE NAVAL AND FAMILY K. ROAD

A few years ago, most of the band at The N and F were elderly and played Victor Sylvester's sort of music. Most of the patrons were also of that vintage and the dances were foxtrots and waltzes. The gentlemen led the ladies back to their seats and pecked a decorous kiss. There were always a lot of Polynesians, who danced superbly and transformed the foxtrots into frenzied mixtures of jive and hula. The dance floor was miniscule and flanked on one side by a big floor-to-ceiling mirror.

By tacit consent, everyone cleared the floor when a solo virtuoso dancer or couple began to perform.

It was thrilling to watch them dance themselves into a trance-like ecstasy – always admiring every twist, turn, thrust and shake in the big mirror opposite.

These days The N. and F. has very good jazz nights and the music seems all the better for the red velvet curtains, the spotlighting and that multiplying mirror.

THE NAVAL AND FAMILY PUB. K. ROAD

'The N and F' is the oldest pub on K. Road now that the old Caledonia has been demolished to make way for the new Sheraton Hotel.

It calls itself a family pub and it has that feeling. The public bar downstairs has all the noise and smoke of a pre-war East End London pub.

A visiting Irish actor from The Abbey Theatre I met, said it was the only place in Auckland he felt comfortable enough to drink in.

He was a little leprechaun of a man and usually sat telling his yarns to an elderly lady to whom he still sends letters from Ireland.

I saw the tallest and most flamboyant transvestite I have ever seen in The N. and F. public bar – about six foot three in stilletto heels and lurex mini skirt, with flaming orange hair and every bit of it shaking away to the juke box.

LOTTERY TICKET SELLER
K. ROAD

What is exotic to one man is mundane to another and the visitor and the visited eye each other with similar reactions.

I have seen Asian tourists photographing these little booths with the same gusto that we pounce on the kerbside cooks and performers of Asia.

The posters covering these booths have a florid uniqueness that comes from trying to make a large amount of money look even larger.

Dollar signs and numerals snake and writhe around in clashing raw colours and are cunningly combined with any motif that relates to the lottery: – Whale of a chance! (whale sprouting dollars) Lucky dip!, (man eyeing voluptuous skinny-dipper!).

I knew an artist who did these for extra money. At first he said he loathed them but gradually the outlandish garishness of them captivated him.

THE WHITE FISH SHOP
K. ROAD

In the days when 'The Pink Pussy Cat' was the 'Wonderful world of Burlesque', the White Fish Shop sold everything that swam or moved in New Zealand waters.

Its windows were a sort of fishy curiosity shop. Because it also sold poultry, local comedians remarked that you got the dead birds here and the live ones next door at the Pink Pussy.

It used to have some beautiful stained glass decorative panels depicting bizarre pop-eyed fish gliding through waving weeds and blowing lovely iridescent bubbles.

Today's White Fish Shop is more streamlined, not so copiously or exotically stocked and the glass panels have gone.

THE NEW WINE BAR
K. ROAD

The new wine bar seems to me schizophrenic. They talk affectionately of the old wine bar rather as one might talk of one's great grandfather who was an axe murderer. They have kept the lights, the Turkington murals, the toilet fixtures, but it needs imagination to see the old place. The new wine bar is curvy art deco, lengthened and broadened by mirrors. A Burgundy costs $1.10 a glass and is served by slightly disdainful young men.

The new management is reported to be not interested in the trendies, who change their haunts overnight, and is looking for wine bar people in the 17 to 70 age group. Time will sort all that out but by then perhaps some interior decorator may have mocked up with the help of old photographs, something that looks like the old wine bar. It's a sort of alcoholic Ann Hathaway's cottage problem.

There is good food available and the wine is excellent and maybe if one got to know the regulars it could be a fun place too.

THE DOMINION WINE BAR –
K. ROAD

It is very hard for *aficionados* to defend the old Wine Bar. It was undeniably dingy, narrow, ill lit, frequented by some *outré* characters and the wine was very cheap but not the stuff for connoisseurs. I discovered it when a single Burgundy cost sixpence and everyone grumbled bitterly about it.

It intrigued me that everyone had a title. There was 'George the Birdman', 'Tom the World Traveller', 'Mick the R.S.M.' and 'High Kicking Lil'. 'The Birdman' sometimes brought his budgie in a cardboard box along and let it out for a fly around.

'High Kicking Lil' could high kick her way the length of the winebar when she was near eighty.

'Fred the Dog Man' toured New Zealand with a troup of performing poodles. 'Stream of Consciousness Tom' never spoke two connected sentences and claimed to operate the traffic lights by some method of mind control. I met people who spoke fluent Urdu and another who claimed to have been a chum of Sinatra.

Members who travelled overseas sent postcards back to the wine bar where they were displayed along with the framed photograph of Cat – a black one who lived on the premises, sipped sherry and grew fat on everyones' leftovers.

It fascinated a lot of very diverse, interesting people and it horrified a lot more.

PARNELL

Les Harvey's Parnell village is certainly going. It is
maybe the hardest place in Auckland to get parking
on a Saturday morning. A local photographer once
told me the amount of colour film bought in Parnell
on the average Saturday, and it was astronomical.

Les's Parnell is an enchanted hotch-potch of
nostalgia and never-never land. So many finials! So
much cobblestone! I believe Parnell was the first
place in Auckland to have a Meat Boutique.

The original Parnell is mostly gone. A little lingers
on, sagging, unpainted, undiscovered in little back
streets to remind us that this was one of Auckland's
first suburbs. Sections went on sale in 1841.

Appropriately this stretch of whimsy is the hub of
Auckland's advertising industry – our very own
Madison Avenue.

It has lots of elegantly restored pubs, where you can
hear the experts talking about ten second
commercials in a jargon usually reserved for
discussions of film masterpieces by *avant garde*
critics.

There are also lots of places to wine and dine
clients. Most of them are small and contrive to look
casual, matey and Left-Bankish with menus
scrawled on black-boards. I'd love to hear what a
real ploughman would say about the price of a lunch
at one of them.

OLD PARNELL

Well, not quite gone, but you have to look for it in the little streets behind the advertising agencies and boutiques.

There are some lovely old houses to remind you that this was the fashionable place to live long before Les Harvey got to work.

It has always intrigued me that Hugh Walpole, that most English of novelists, was born in Parnell.

OTARA OPEN MARKET

All the amateur sociologists I know, and that includes most of the people I know, cite Otara as "A typical example" of a certain type of community.

They also usually contrast it unfavourably with their own. All I know for certain about Otara is that it has a splendid public library, exciting murals on the community centre's walls and a big thriving open market every Saturday morning.

There are many parts of Auckland that, by design or accident, feel like somewhere in the northern latitudes, but Otara's market smells, looks and sounds like I hoped the South Pacific would.

81

STREET PEOPLE

Street kids, walkers, musicians and traders have all proliferated in Auckland over the past four years. The Hare Krishnas created a furore when they first arrived chanting and singing up and down Queen Street, but now most people would miss their colourful contribution to city life.

The first punk rockers also made a sensation but green hair and safety pinned ears don't turn many heads today.

The singing cowboy and the jewellery sellers are part of the scenery and Queen Street would feel incomplete without the flower seller shrilling, "Wanna buy a pretty flower lady", usually followed up with "What's your telephone number lady!"

I keep seeing things on the streets to remind me that nothing we can invent can compete with reality for poignancy or humour.

There was the little old lady singing hymns on Karangahape Road one rainy Christmas Eve. She was accompanied by a long-haired hippy-looking young man who played blues chords on his guitar and responded with a bass profundo voice, "Yeah, yeah!, Tell it man, Tell it!"

Or another very handsome young man who juggled coloured balls in Albert Park, not for money but "For the glory of it".

Not forgetting the two intense young musicians standing in a doorway on Queen Street playing Mozart.

THANK YOU